DOVER · THRIFT · EDITIONS

Electra

SOPHOCLES

DOVER PUBLICATIONS, INC.
New York

DOVER THRIFT EDITIONS

GENERAL EDITOR: STANLEY APPELBAUM
EDITOR OF THIS VOLUME: THOMAS CROFTS

Published in Canada by General Publishing Company, Ltd., 30 Lesmill Road, Don Mills, Toronto, Ontario.

Published in the United Kingdom by Constable and Company, Ltd., 3 The Lanchesters, 162–164 Fulham Palace Road, London W6 9ER.

Bibliographical Note

This Dover edition, first published in 1995, is an unabridged republication of the play *Electra* from the volume *The Dramas of Sophocles Rendered in English Verse Dramatic & Lyric by Sir George Young*, as published by J. M. Dent & Sons, Ltd., London, in 1906. (The Dent edition was the second, the first having been published by George Bell & Sons, London, in 1888.) See the new Note, specially written for the Dover edition, for further details.

Library of Congress Cataloging-in-Publication Data

Sophocles.
   [Electra. English]
   Electra / Sophocles ; translated by Sir George Young.
      p.   cm—(Dover thrift editions)
   ISBN 0-486-28482-4 (pbk.)
   1. Electra (Greek mythology)—Drama.   I. Young, George, Sir, 1837–1930.
II. Title.   III. Series.
PA4414.E5Y68   1995
882'.01—dc20
                                               94-44867
                                                CIP

Manufactured in the United States of America
Dover Publications, Inc., 31 East 2nd Street, Mineola, N.Y. 11501

Note

SOPHOCLES (born ca. 496 B.C., died after 413) was one of the three masters of tragic theater flourishing in 5th-century Athens. He wrote 123 plays, only seven of which survive. *Electra* was written and first performed in the late 440s.

Unlike most of the violence we experience in dramatic form these days, the bloodshed of Sophocles' stage is always the issue of intense emotional agony, and signifies nothing less than the psychological rebirth of the hero. In perhaps the most well-known of Sophocles' plays, *Oedipus Rex*, the young hero enters his destiny only after killing his father, and fulfills it by blinding himself. His destiny is of course an unhappy one, but happiness is not the goal of a Sophoclean protagonist. The goal is a cataclysmic overthrow of circumstance. Oedipus was drawn by the irresistible forces of his own nature, the justice of his deeds being beside the point (as they were inadvertent.) In Sophocles' universe, nature is stacked, long before the participant is aware of it, in such a way that a character's personality must be pushed almost to the point of dementia before his decisive act becomes clear. While this understanding might also be extended to the *antagonists* of the plays, for they too do bloody deeds, the hero always lacks the outright criminality of the antagonist, whose acts put the tragic mechanism into motion. In these respects, poor Hamlet of Elsinore is a hero very much in the Sophoclean vein.

In *Electra*, the trouble brewing is in Argos, in the house of Agamemnon Atréides, who, returning victorious from the Trojan War, was (before the present action begins) murdered by his wife Clytaemnestra and Aegisthus, her lover. Aegisthus, then, fearing that Agamemnon's young son Orestes would one day avenge his father's murder, made plans to have the boy killed too. This would have been accomplished had not

the boy's older sister Electra taken care to send him away, to friends
outside of Argos, so that he might safely grow to maturity. Meanwhile,
Electra and her sister Chrysothemis remained under their mother and
new father's roof, in full knowledge of their crime, for several years until
the time of this play's beginning. Now, as Electra has hoped that he
would, Orestes returns. Electra has kept her grief fresh over the years,
and laments her father's murder as inconsolably as ever. Her refusal to
accept the situation as it is, her fiery demeanor, symbolize the *necessity*
of Orestes' mission, as, accompanied by his old guardian and his good
friend Pylades, he comes home to reckon with his family's bloody
circumstances.

The translation by Sir George Young (1837–1930) is not only very
accurate; it also preserves the feeling of the original Greek to a great
extent. The verse forms are reasonable English equivalents; the
diction — lightly archaic in the blank-verse dialogues, heightened and
more involuted in the stanzaic choruses — admirably reflects the hier-
atic nature of Sophocles' drama.

In the present edition, Sir George's own notes (exclusively concerned
with problems of the Greek text and its interpretation) have been
omitted. Several new, brief footnotes have been added, clarifying some
allusions for readers less familiar with classical mythology and lore.

ELECTRA

Persons Represented

ORESTES, *son of Agamemnon, the late king of Argos and Mycenæ, and of Clytæmnestra.*

PYLADES, *friend to Orestes.*

An old Attendant, Guardian to Orestes.

ELECTRA,   } *daughters of Agamemnon and*
CHRYSOTHEMIS, } *Clytæmnestra.*

CLYTÆMNESTRA, *queen of Argos and Mycenæ.*

ÆGISTHUS, *cousin to Agamemnon, and in his lifetime the paramour of Clytæmnestra.*

The Chorus is composed of Ladies of Mycenæ, friends to Electra.

Attendants on Clytæmnestra.

ELECTRA

Scene, before the Palace at Mycenæ.

Enter ORESTES, PYLADES *and Guardian.*

GUARDIAN.   Son of our Captain in the wars of Troy,
  Great Agamemnon, it is given thee now
  With thine own eyes, Orestes, to behold
  Those scenes thou hast ever longed for. Here it lies,
  Argos, the ancient land of thy desire;
  The sacred glade of her the gadfly drave,
  Inachus' daughter;* that's the Agora
  They call Lycean, from the wolf-slaying God;
  This, on the left, Hera's renowned fane;
  And from the point we are reaching you can swear
  You see Mycenæ's Golden City, and this,
  The death-fraught house of Pelops' family;
  Whence I received you at your sister's hands,
  And saved you from the slaughter of your sire,
  And carried you away, and fostered you
  So far toward manhood, ready to revenge
  A father's blood. Wherefore, Orestes, now —
  And Pylades, thou dearest of allies —
  Take we brief counsel what is right to do;

---

* Io, daughter of the river god Inachus, became attractive to Zeus, thereby incurring the wrath of Hera, who changed her into a cow, and set a stinging insect upon her which drove her out of Argos.

For see, already the bright gleam of day
Calls up the birds to sing their matins clear
Above us, and the sable star-lit night
Has passed away. Now, before any man
Comes forth abroad, join you in conference;
For where we stand, it is no season more
To hesitate; the hour is come for action.

ORESTES.   My faithfullest of followers, what clear signs
You manifest of your good will to us!
For as a generous steed, though he be old,
Beset with difficulties, pricks his ears
And bates not of his courage, you impart
Spirit to us, and lag no whit behind.
As you desire, I will unfold my scheme;
Do you the while mark my words heedfully,
And if I miss the target, mend my aim.
Late, when I sought the Pythian oracle,
To learn how I might execute revenge
Upon my father's murderers, Phœbus gave me
Answer in this sort; I will tell it you;
I by myself unarmed with shields and martial bands
By craft held condign slaughter hidden in my hands.
Well, with this answer sounding in our ears,
Go you, as opportunity may lead,
Into the house, and gather all that passes,
And bring us word of all; for in old age,
And so long after, they will never know
Now, nor suspect you, frosted thus by time.
Tell your tale thus; you are a citizen
Of Phocis, and you come from Phanoteus,
Who is their best ally; tell them (and swear it)
Orestes has been killed by accident,
By a fall from his chariot, at the Pythian games;
Let it stand so. We, as He bade, the while,
First with libations and shorn curls of hair
Will deck my father's grave; then back again
Return, carrying an urn of beaten brass,

(The same, you know, that in the brake lies hidden,)
That in feigned words we may convey to them
Glad tidings — how my body is destroyed,
Burnt up already and made embers of!
For where's the harm to be called dead, when really
I am alive, and gather praise thereby?
No word that profits us can hurt, I fancy.
Why, I have seen men often, who were wise,
Falsely pretending death; then, when again
They came back home, they have been more prized than ever;
So I expect yet, out of this report,
To blaze forth, star-like, living, on my foes.
But O my native land! Gods of the soil!
Welcome me with good fortune in these ways;
And thou, paternal Home! for I thy cleanser
Come here of right, the ambassador of Heaven;
Send me not with dishonour from this land,
But grant me to inherit and set up
The old estate. — I have spoken. Now, old friend,
Be it your care to guard your post; go forward;
And let us forth. It is the season; this,
In every action, is men's best ally.

ELECTRA (*within*). Ah woe is me!

GUARDIAN.   Hark!
I thought I heard some handmaiden cry faintly
Inside the doors, my son!

ORESTES.   Is it perhaps
The wronged Electra? Shall we stay awhile
And listen to her sorrowing?

GUARDIAN.   By no means.
Do nothing ere performing what is bidden
Of Loxias,* and initiate all from thence,

---

* Epithet of Apollo, meaning either *the Ambiguous* or *the Speaker*.

Pouring lustrations on your father's grave.
This wafts us victory, and nerves our doings.   [*Exeunt.*

Enter ELECTRA.

ELECTRA.   Holy Light, with Earth, and Sky,
    Whom thou fillest equally,
    Ah how many a note of woe,
    Many a self-inflicted blow
    On my scarred breast might'st thou mark,
    Ever as recedes the dark;
    Known, too, all my nightlong cheer
    To bitter bed and chamber drear,
    How I mourn my father lost,
    Whom on no barbarian coast
        Did red Ares greet amain,
    But as woodmen cleave an oak
    My mother's axe dealt murderous stroke,
    Backed by the partner of her bed,
    Fell Ægisthus, on his head;
    Whence no pity, save from me,
    O my father, flows for thee,
        So falsely, foully slain.
    Yet I will not cease from sighing,
    Cease to pour my bitter crying,
    While I see this light of day,
    Or the stars' resplendent play,
    Uttering forth a sound of wail,
    Like the child-slayer, the nightingale,*
    Here before my father's door
    Crying to all men evermore.
    O Furies dark, of birth divine!
    O Hades wide, and Proserpine!
        Thou nether Hermes! Ara great!†

---

* Philomela, who, with Procne, killed Tereus' son Itys, cooked him and served him to his
  father.
† Ara: goddess of destruction and revenge.

Ye who regard the untimely dead,
The dupes of an adulterous bed,
Come ye, help me, and require
The foul murder of our sire;
And send my brother back again;
Else I may no more sustain
    Grief's overmastering weight.

Enter Chorus of Ladies of Mycenæ.

CHORUS.   O child, Electra, child
Of one too fatally bold,
How sighest thou, unsatisfied yet,
Evermore wasting away,
For him, Agamemnon, beguiled
By thy crafty mother of old,
Spite of all Gods, in her net,
To base hands given for a prey?
Accurst be the author of this!
    If I pray not amiss.

ELECTRA.   O women of noble strain,
Ye are come to solace my pain;
I know it, I well perceive;
It escapes me not at all;
Howbeit I will not leave
To lament my father's fall.
Ye my love who repay
With all love ever gave,
Ah let me be, I pray,
    Leave me to rave.

CHORUS.   But not from Hades below,
Not from the all-welcoming shore,
Even with strong crying and prayer
Canst thou raise thy father again.
Past all measure in woe
Thou art perishing evermore,

Sinking deep in despair,
Where no release is from pain;
Ah why so bent upon grief,
        Too sore for relief?

ELECTRA.   None but fools could forget
        Their fathers' wrongs, who are gone.
        But on her my fancy is set,
        The bird, Heaven's messenger,
        Wildly bemoaning her
        For Itys, Itys alone!
        O forlorn Niobe,*
        As one godlike I deem of thee,
        Alas! that abidest, weeping,
                In a rock-tomb's keeping!

CHORUS.   Not first of mortals with thee,
        Daughter, did sorrow begin;
        Whereas thou passest the rest,
        Thy kith and kindred within,
        The life Chrysothemis lives,
        And Iphianassa, and he
        In the flower of his youth who grieves,
        Hid, but not all unblest,
        Whom the land, Mycenæ fair,
        Will receive, her princes' heir,
        When he, Orestes, shall come
                By Heaven's guidance home.

ELECTRA.   Whom I wait for, and go
        Ceaselessly wet with tears,
        Unespoused, childless, forlorn,
        Bearing still, as I must,
        The unending burden of woe;
        But he forgets with the years

---

* Boastful, blasphemous woman whose fourteen children were wiped out by Apollo and
  Artemis. She had claimed to be more fertile than their mother Leto. Niobe herself was
  turned to stone.

All he has heard and borne;
For what message comes I can trust?
Ever he longs to be here —
    He will not appear!

CHORUS.   Nay cheer thee, cheer thee, my child;
    God in the Heavens is yet great,
    Who surveys all else and commands.
    Leave thou then in his hands
    Anger — the excess of regret,
    Nor chide overmuch — nor forget
    Those whom thou needs must hate.
    For Time is a God right mild;
    Nor can Agamemnon's son
    By Crisa's pastoral shore,
    Nor the monarch of Acheron,
        Be deaf evermore.

ELECTRA.   But already most of my day,
    Hopeless, has faded away;
    I can do no longer withal;
    Without parents to cherish me I waste,
    Without husband's love, to defend;
    Yea alien-like, disgraced,
    I inhabit my father's hall,
    And in this guise attend
    At a board with no feast laid,
        Uncomely arrayed.

CHORUS.   At his return arose
    A burden of woes — of woes
    To thy father's resting-place,
    What time was darted a thrust,
    From fangs all brass, at his face.
    Fraud was deviser — Lust
    Was slayer — embodying the shade
    Of a fell deed foully planned,

       Yea, whether by heavenly aid
          Or a mortal's hand.

ELECTRA.   O day that far beyond all
      Dawned most hateful to see!
      O night — O sorrows abhorred
      Of that ghastly festival —
      Murder done villainously
      On my sire, by the hands of twain
      Who took my life as a prey,
      Who annihilated me!
      Whom may God with rightful reward,
      The Olympian Power, again
      For their deeds amply repay,
      Nor let them compass their bliss
          By an act like this!

CHORUS.   Take heed; say no more.
      Hast thou no consciousness
      Out of what wealth before
      Thou fall'st thus miserably
      Into ills that abide with thee?
      Thou hast wrought thee woes in excess,
      Bringing forth strife on strife
      To the heaviness of thy life;
      And is it so easy a thing
          To contend with a king?

ELECTRA.   Hard is my fate, full hard;
      I know it; I am mad, I confess;
      Yet not for the fates that oppress
      Will I keep this wrath under guard,
      The while my life shall endure!
      For from whom, companions dear,
      Should I submissively hear
      Reason, or from whom, that is wise,
      Counsel, fit for mine ear?
      Let me be; cease to advise;

All this must pass without cure;
I shall never be free from distress,
     And laments numberless.

CHORUS.   Yet I bid thee, faithful still,
As a mother, and in good will,
Do not add new ill unto ill.

ELECTRA.   And where should a limit be set
          For evil to spread?
Or how is it well, to forget
          The cause of the dead?
In what man's heart
          Could a plant like this find place?
Be mine no part
          In such men's favour or grace!
Nor, if with any good things
          My fortune is blent,
Be it mine to rest in content,
          And fetter the wings
Of piercing cries, or tire,
          Praising my sire.
For if in the earth, as nought,
          The dead must lie,
And these, in return, who ought,
          The slayers, not die,
Then farewell honour, and fall
          Men's reverence, all!

I LADY.   I came, my daughter, zealous for your good
As for my own; but if I say not well,
Have it your way; for we will follow you.

ELECTRA.   I am ashamed, dear ladies, if to you
Through frequent lamentations I appear
Too sorely oppressed; but, for necessity
Obliges me to do so, pardon me.
For how should any woman gently born,
Viewing the sorrows of her father's house,

Do otherwise than I, who witness them
For ever day by day and night by night
Rather increase than lessen? to whom, first,
The mother's face who bare me has become
Most hostile; next, I must be companied
In my own home with my sire's murderers,
By them be ruled, take at their hands, or else
At their hands hunger! Then, what sort of days
Do you suppose I lead, when I behold
Ægisthus seated on my father's throne,
Wearing the selfsame garments which he wore,
And pouring out libations on the hearth
By which he slew him? When I witness, too,
The consummation of their impudence,
The homicide lying in my father's bed
With that abandoned mother — if it be right
To call her mother, who consorts with him!
And she — so profligate that she lives on
With her blood-guilty mate — fearing no vengeance —
Rather, as if exulting in her doings —
Looks out the day on which by cunning erst
She slew my father, and each month on it
Sets dances going, and sacrifices sheep
In offering to her guardian deities!
I see it, I, ill-fated one! At home
I weep and waste and sorrow as I survey
The unblest feast that bears my father's name,
In private; for I cannot even weep
So freely as my heart would have me do;
For this tongue-valiant woman with vile words
Upbraids me, crying "Thou God-forsaken thing,
Has no man's father died, save only thine?
Is nobody in mourning, except thee?
Ill death betide thee, and the nether Gods
Give thee no end to these thy sorrowings!"
So she reviles; save when she hears it said
Orestes is at hand; then instantly

She is possest, and comes and screams at me—
"Is it not you who are the cause of this?
Pray is not this your doing, who stole Orestes
Out of my hands, and conjured him away?
But mind you, you shall pay me well for it!"
So snarling, there joins with her and stands by
And hounds her forward her illustrious groom,
The all unmanly, all injurious pest,
Who fights no battles without women! I,
Waiting and waiting, till Orestes come
And end it, miserably daily die.
For always meaning, never doing, he
Has utterly confounded all my hopes
Remote or present. Friends, in such a case,
There is no room—no, not for soberness
Or piety; but, beneath injuries,
There is deep need we prove injurious, too!

1 LADY.   Stay, tell me, is it with Ægisthus near
You talk thus to us, or is he gone from home?

ELECTRA.   That is he. Never think, if he were by,
I could roam forth; but he is abroad just now.

1 LADY.   Then I might come with better confidence
To speech of you, that being so.

ELECTRA.   Oh, ask freely;
He is not here. What do you want to know?

1 LADY.   And so I will. What of your brother say you?
I would fain know, will he come soon, or tarry?

ELECTRA.   He says he will. He does not keep his word.

1 LADY.   A man is backward, when on some great exploit.

ELECTRA.   I was not backward, when I rescued him!

1 LADY.   Take courage, he is of a worthy stock;
He will not fail his friends.

ELECTRA.   I trust so. Else
     I never should have been alive so long.

I LADY.   Hush, say no more just now; for I perceive
     Chrysothemis your sister, who was born
     Of the same mother and same sire as you,
     Come from the palace, carrying in her hands
     Oblations customary to the dead.

Enter CHRYSOTHEMIS.

CHRYSOTHEMIS.   Sister, what talk is this, you come and cry
     Aloud, abroad, before the outer gate,
     Nor will not learn, taught by long years, to cease
     Vainly indulging unavailing rage?
     I for myself can say as much as this —
     I chafe at those I live with, in such fashion
     As, if I could get power, I would make plain
     The sort of temper that I bear towards them;
     But in these dangers it seems good to sail
     Close-reefed, and not pretend to be at work,
     But effect nothing harmful; and I wish
     You too would do the like; and yet, the right
     Is not as I declare, but as you judge it;
     Still, if I am to live at liberty,
     I must in all things heed my governors.

ELECTRA.   Well, it is strange that you, being his child
     Who was your sire, should have regard for her,
     Your mother, and have quite forgotten him!
     All this good counsel you bestow on me
     Is of her teaching; and of your own self
     You can say nothing. Therefore take your choice;
     Either to be of evil mind, or else
     Well minded to forget those dear to you;
     Who said but now, if you could get the power,
     You would shew plain the hate you have for them;

And yet, while I am doing everything
To avenge our father, do not take your part,
And seek to turn me from it, who take mine!
Danger! Is there not cowardice as well?
Come, answer me, what should it profit me
To cease my mourning? Or else hear me speak;
Do I not live? unprosperously I know,
But well enough for me; to them, the while,
I am a torment, and so render honour
To him that's gone, if there be service there!
You — madam hatress — you pretend you hate,
But really take your father's murderers' side!
For my part, I will never bend to them;
Not though a man should come and offer me
These gauds of yours, in which you glory now!
Yours be the full-spread board, the cup o'erflowing;
For me — be it my only sustenance
Not to offend against my conscience. Thus,
I do not ask to share your dignities,
And were you well-advised, no more would you!
But now, though it be in your power to be called
Your father's child — the foremost of mankind,
Be called — your mother's! So you shall appear
In most men's eyes unmeritoriously,
False to your friends, and to your father's shade.

I LADY.   Now in Heaven's name, no chiding! There is good
In what you both have said, if you would learn
Something from her, and she, in turn, from you.

CHRYSOTHEMIS.   Oh, I am quite accustomed to her talk;
Nor, ladies, had I ever said one word,
Had I not heard a very great mishap
Was coming on her, which will make her cease
From her long sorrowing.

ELECTRA.   Come, your bug-bear, tell it!

If you can mention any greater grief
Than these I have, I will reply no more.

CHRYSOTHEMIS. Well, I will tell you everything I know.
They are going, if you will not cease this mourning,
To send you where you will not any more
See daylight, but sing sorrow underground,
Buried alive, out of this territory.
Wherefore take heed, or by and by, in trouble
Never blame me. Prudence is easy, now.

ELECTRA. Ay? have they purposed to do so to me?

CHRYSOTHEMIS. Most surely, when Ægisthus shall come home.

ELECTRA. Why as for that, let him come speedily!

CHRYSOTHEMIS. What was it that you prayed for, silly one?

ELECTRA. For him to come; if he is that way minded.

CHRYSOTHEMIS. So you may get — what treatment? Are you mad?

ELECTRA. So I may get — farthest away from you!

CHRYSOTHEMIS. And of life present have you no regard?

ELECTRA. Living like mine is choice, to marvel at!

CHRYSOTHEMIS. It might be, had you sense to be discreet.

ELECTRA. Do not instruct me to be treacherous.

CHRYSOTHEMIS. I do not; but to yield to those who govern.

ELECTRA. Well, gloze it so; you do not speak my language.

CHRYSOTHEMIS. Yet it were well not to be ruined through folly.

ELECTRA. Come ruin, if needful, in a father's quarrel!

CHRYSOTHEMIS. I am sure our father pardons us for this.

ELECTRA. That is the speech a villain might approve.

CHRYSOTHEMIS. You will not hearken and agree with me?

ELECTRA.   I trust I am not yet so senseless. No!

CHRYSOTHEMIS.   Then I will go on whither I was sent.

ELECTRA.   Where are you going? To whom bear you these offerings?

CHRYSOTHEMIS.   My mother sends me, to strew my father's grave.

ELECTRA.   How say you? To the most detested foe —

CHRYSOTHEMIS.   Yes — "whom she murdered!" That is what you mean?

ELECTRA.   By whom, of all friends, bidden? At whose desire?

CHRYSOTHEMIS.   Through some nocturnal panic, to my thinking.

ELECTRA.   God of my fathers, only aid me now!

CHRYSOTHEMIS.   Do you gain any courage from her scare?

ELECTRA.   Tell me about the dream, and I could say.

CHRYSOTHEMIS.   Only I do not know it; except just
In brief, the story.

ELECTRA.   Well, but tell me that;
Brief words ere now have often led astray —
And righted mortals.

CHRYSOTHEMIS.   It is said she saw
An apparition of your sire and mine
Come back again to daylight; and he took
The sceptre which he sometime bore himself,
But now Ægisthus bears, and planted it
Upon the hearth, and out of it a shoot
Budded and grew, till all Mycenæ's land
Was covered with its shadow. So I heard
Related by a fellow who was by,
While to the Sun-God she disclosed her dream.
But more than this I know not; only that
She sends me on account of this alarm.
Now I beseech you, by our country's Gods,

Listen to me, and be not ruined by folly;
For though you should repulse me, by and by
In trouble you will turn to me again.

ELECTRA.   Nay but let nothing of your fardel, dear,
Light on the tomb! for it were shame — were sin
From an abominable spouse to bring
Lustrations near, or perform obsequies
To a sire's shade. Let the winds have them, rather!
Or hide them deep in dust, where none of them
Shall ever touch our father's resting-place;
Let them be kept, stored underground, for her
When she is dead! Why, if she were not grown
The most abandoned of all womankind,
She never would have dreamt of smothering
With her unfriendly strewments him she murdered!
Why look you, think you the entombed dead
Will take these gifts in kindness, at her hands
Who slew him foully, like an enemy,
Lopped of the extremities, the stains of blood
Smeared off, for lustral washings, on his head!
Do you imagine what you bear can purge
Her from her murder? Never! Let it be!
Cut from your head the longest locks of hair —
And mine, unhappy — small the gift, indeed,
But what I have — and give it him, this hair
Untended, and my girdle, unadorned
With broiderings! Fall upon your knees, and pray him
In favour come and help us, from the earth,
Against our enemies; and that his boy
Orestes may set foot, before he die,
Superior, on the bodies of his foes,
That we may crown him afterward with hands
Larger in gift than we can proffer now!
Yea I believe, I do believe, that he
Had part in sending her this ugly dream;
But still, sister, do this, for your own good,

And mine, and his, the man of all mankind
Dearest, our sire, who in the grave lies dead.

1 LADY.   The princess speaks religiously, my friend;
And you, if you are wise, will heed her.

CHRYSOTHEMIS.   Yes.
It stands to reason, not that two should quarrel
Over their duty, but be quick and do it.
Only while I essay this business, friends,
Do you keep secret, in the name of Heaven!
For if my mother hears it, to my cost,
Methinks, I shall attempt this venture, yet.
                              [*Exit* CHRYSOTHEMIS.

CHORUS.

I.

If I be seer
Not wholly erring and unpolicied,
Self-prophesying Justice means to appear,
Bringing large succour to the righteous side,
And following on, my child, with no long waiting-tide.
Courage springs up within me, as I hear
The voice of dreams, breathing sweet music near;
He who begat thee, the Hellenian King,
Forgets not ever; nor that Ancient Thing,
The two-edged brazen fang, by which he foully died.

2.

Lo, this is she,
Erinys,* hiding her dread ambushed bands,
Sandalled with brass, with myriad feet and hands.
Yea time hath been, when they who should not, plied
A blood-stained spousal-work, unmeet for bed or bride.
Whence it comes o'er me, I shall never see

---

* Collective name for the Eumenides, or Furies.

On doer and accomplice harmlessly
This portent fall; and nothing future can
By good or ill dream be revealed to man,
If this night-vision speed not, landward, on the tide.

O chariot-race weary
Of Pelops of old,
How fateful, how dreary,
Thou hast proved to this land!
For since Myrtilus slumbered,
From the chariot, all gold,
Torn, silenced for ever,
Flung far from the strand,
From thenceforth never
The weary disgrace
Of troubles unnumbered
Hath passed from the race.

Enter CLYTÆMNESTRA, *attended.*

CLYTÆMNESTRA.   You gad abroad, then, masterless again,
Ægisthus absent; who did hinder you
From bringing scandal on your family
By brawling at the doors! Now he is gone,
You pay no heed to me; though many a time,
In many people's ears, you have proclaimed —
I, without shame or warrant, violate
Your rights and honours! I meanwhile commit
No violence; I but repay with scorn
The scorn you heap on me. Your father, though —
This and no other — is your pretext still,
How by my hand he died! By mine; I know it;
There's no denial of the deed in me.
But Justice slew him; I was not alone;
And had you sense, you ought to take her side;
Since he, this father whom you still bewail,

Alone of all the Argives had the heart
To offer to the Gods your sister's life —
Whose pains in her begetting equalled not
My travail-pangs, who bare her! Be it so;
Now tell me for what cause, and for whose sake,
He offered her? For the Argives, will you say?
They had no right to kill a child of mine!
If for his brother Menelaus' sake
He slew my daughter, was not he to pay
Forfeit for that? Were there not children twain
Born to that father, who, had right been done,
Ought rather to have died, whose sire and dam
Themselves had caused that voyage? Had the Grave
Some fancy for my offspring, for its feast,
Rather than hers? Or had all natural love
Expired in that pernicious father's heart
For children born of me, but not for children
Of Menelaus? Was it not the act
Of a perverse insensate sire? I think it,
Though you deny; and so would that dead girl
Say, could she speak. For what my hands have done
I do not feel remorse; but if to you
I seem of evil mind, censure your folk,
When you yourself are just!

ELECTRA.   You cannot say
    Now, that I crossed you and you answered me!
    Yet if you gave me scope, I would speak fairly
    For him that's dead, and for my sister too.

CLYTÆMNESTRA.   I give it you! If you addressed me thus
    Always, it would not chafe me so to hear.

ELECTRA.   Then listen! You avow my father's death;
    What could more ill become your mouth than this,
    Whether he were unjustly slain or no?

But let me tell you that you slew him not
For Justice, but perverted by the lure
Of a base wretch, who is your consort now.
What! Question of the Huntress Artemis
On whose account she held the various winds
Spell-bound in Aulis! Rather, I will tell;
For 'tis not given you to learn of her.
My father once, as I have heard the tale,
While sporting in a sacred wood of hers,
Roused as he went a dappled antlered roe,
And with some careless vaunt of slaughtering it
Shoots at and hits it; wherefore Leto's maid,
Wrathful at this, kept back the Achaian host,
Till he should render up for sacrifice,
In payment for the beast, his daughter dear —
And therefore was she offered; since escape
There was none other for the armament,
Either toward Ilium, or backward home.
Whence much enforced, and much resisting it,
Not for the sake of Menelaus, he
Unwillingly gave her to the knife at last.
But what an if (for I will take your story)
He did it through benevolence for him?
Was it thereafter just that he should perish,
And at your hand? Under what law? Beware
You do not, while you set this law to others,
Lay up repentance for yourself, and pain.
If we begin to exchange life for life,
You should die next, if you received your due.
But look you do not proffer for excuse
That which is not; for tell me, if you will,
Why you are now doing things most execrable,
Consorting with the branded murderer
By whose connivance erst you slew my sire,
And bearing children, to the extrusion of
Your honest first-born, born in honesty?
How should I pardon this? Or will you claim

In this, too, to be trying to avenge
Your daughter? It sounds vilely, if you do;
For 'twere unseemly in a daughter's quarrel
To couple with an enemy! Ay truly,
It's an offence even to admonish you,
Who let your tongue run freely, when you say
That I speak evil of my mother! I
A slave-mistress account you, over us,
As much as mother; for a servile life
Is that I lead, compassed with many griefs,
Wrought by yourself and by your paramour.
And poor Orestes is an exile, too,
Hardly delivered from your violence,
And living on in wretchedness—the same
You have so oft charged me with nurturing
To take revenge on you; and so I would—
Never doubt that—if I were strong enough.
Now, for that treason, publish me to all
Shameless—perverse—abusive—what you will;
And if I be an adept in the same,
I do bare justice to your blood in me!

1 LADY.   I see her breathing fury! Right or wrong,
     Now, 'tis all one, for any thought she gives it!

CLYTÆMNESTRA.   What sort of thought, then, must I give to her,
     Who in this fashion dares insult her mother,
     And at her years? Do you suppose she means
     To exceed all measure in her shamelessness?

ELECTRA.   Now understand, I do feel shame at this,
     Although to you I may not seem to feel it.
     I do perceive that I am doing things
     Unseasonable, and unbefitting me.
     Only your acts and your hostility
     Force me to this behaviour. Infamy
     Is got by contact with the infamous.

CLYTÆMNESTRA.   Insolent creature! I, my words and acts,
    Make you so loudly over-eloquent?

ELECTRA.   It is your fault, not mine; you are the doer,
    And deeds find names.

CLYTÆMNESTRA.   Now not by Artemis,
    Who is my mistress, when Ægisthus comes
    Shall you escape, for this audacity!

ELECTRA.   See, now you fly into a frenzy! First
    You let me speak my mind — then, you'll not listen!

CLYTÆMNESTRA.   Will you not let me sacrifice, without
    Words of ill omen, after suffering you
    To say all that you can?

ELECTRA.   Go, sacrifice!
    I let you! Nay, I bid you! Censure not
    My mouth again, for I shall say no more.

CLYTÆMNESTRA.   Take up the offerings, you that wait on me,
    The fruits of earth, that unto this my Lord
    I may prefer petitions for release
    Out of my present terrors. — Hear thou now,
    Protector Phœbus, my unuttered vow!
    For what I say I say not among friends,
    Nor is it meet to uncover all my ends
    Here, in her presence, to the open sky,
    Lest she with malice and loud clamorous cry
    Scatter vain babblings to the city round;
    But softly list, and soft my words shall sound.
    The ambiguous visions, whose dim shadowing
    Last night I witnessed, O Lycean King,
    If they portended good, give them like close;
    If evil, turn them backward on my foes,
    And do not thou, if any would by stealth,
    Let them disturb me from my present wealth;
    Let me live on securely, as to-day,

Holding the Atridæ's palace, and their sway,
Abiding with the friends I bide withal
Now, in good case; and with my children, all
Through whom no bitter pang is made to strike
Their mother's heart, nor shudder of dislike.
Hear, great Apollo, what I pray for thus,
And, as we ask, in grace give all of us.
— The rest, I think, thou, being divine, perceiv'st,
Though I be silent; for it cannot be
But all is open to the sons of Jove.

Enter Guardian.

GUARDIAN.   Ladies, to whom I am a foreigner,
Pray how might I discover if this palace
Be that of King Ægisthus?

I LADY.   Sir, it is;
Your guess is right.

GUARDIAN.   And am I further right
In guessing that this lady is his wife?
She bears a queenly presence.

I LADY.   Certainly:
You see her there before you.

GUARDIAN.   Madam, hail!
I bring you pleasant tidings from a friend;
You, and Ægisthus also.

CLYTÆMNESTRA.   They are welcome.
But I would hear first, who he was that sent you.

GUARDIAN.   Phanoteus of Phocis, with a weighty charge.

CLYTÆMNESTRA.   Of what sort, stranger, say? for I am sure,
Being from a friend, that you will speak us friendly.

GUARDIAN.   Briefly I speak. Orestes is no more.

ELECTRA.   O I am lost, unhappy!

CLYTÆMNESTRA.   What sir, what?
  Never mind her!

GUARDIAN.   I say as I have said.
  Orestes is dead.

ELECTRA.   O me, I am undone!
  Now I am nothing!

CLYTÆMNESTRA.   Yea, see thou to that.
  How came he by his death, sir? Tell me truly.

GUARDIAN.   I will tell all; for to that end I came.
  The man had gone to the great festival —
  The glory of Hellas — for the Delphian games;
  And when he heard the shouting of the crier
  Calling the foot-race, which is first adjudged,
  He entered for it, comely to behold,
  The worship of the eyes of all men there;
  And having reached the limit of the course
  Whence they were started, he came out of it
  With the all-honoured prize of victory.
  To say but little out of much I might,
  I never saw before the acts and prowess
  Of such a man as he; but take one statement;
  In every heat for which the judges set
  The customary courses, out and home,
  He brought off all the honours of the day,
  And was congratulated, and proclaimed
  "An Argive, named Orestes" — and "the son
  Of Agamemnon," him who mustered once
  The illustrious host of Hellas. So far well.
  But if some Deity is bent on harm,
  It is not even a strong man can escape.
  For he, another day at sunrise, when
  Owners of horses met to try their speed,
  With many other charioteers, went in.

One was Achaian, one from Sparta, two
Libyans, skilled masters of the yoke and car;
He among these, with mares of Thessaly,
Came fifth; the sixth was from Ætolia,
With bright bay colts; the seventh Magnesian;
The eighth of Ænian birth, his horses white;
The ninth from Athens the divinely builded;
Last, a Bœotian's car made up the ten.
These, stationed where the judges of the course
Cast each his lot, and ranked his driving-board,
Forth started at the brazen bugle's note,
And cheering to their horses all at once
Shook the grasped reins; then the whole course was filled
With rattle of the chariot metal-work;
The dust rose high; crowded together, all
Spared not the goad — so might some one of them
Fore-reach on snorting steed and axle-tree;
While evermore alike on back and wheel,
Foaming and quick, the coursers' panting came.
But he kept close under the endmost mark,
Sweeping his axle round continuously,
And, giving rein to the right-handmost steed,
Pulled back the inner goer. And at first
The driving-boards all held themselves upright;
But afterwards the Ænian's hard-mouthed colts
Bolt violently; and coming from the turn,
After the sixth, just in the seventh round,
Dash all their fronts against the Barca car;
Then, in an instant, from one accident,
Car upon car began to crash and fall,
And the whole plain of Crisa became filled
With wreck of steeds and tackling. At the sight
That crafty driver, he from Athens, draws
Out of the way, and slackens, passing by
The surge of chariots eddying in the midst.
Last came Orestes, trusting to the close,
Keeping his fillies back; but seeing him

Left in alone, he launches a shrill whoop
Through his fleet coursers' ears, and races him,
And yoke and yoke the couple drove along,
Now one and now the other shewing head
Out in the front, over their carriages.
Well, all his rounds, poor fellow, till the last,
He stood up straight, and kept his chariot straight,
And drove straight through; then, slackening the left rein
As his horse turns, he struck unwittingly
The corner of the mark, and snapped the nave
Short from the axle, and slipped instantly
Over the rail, and in the cloven reins
Was tangled; as upon the plain he fell,
His steeds into the middle of the course
Ran all astray. Then the whole host, that saw him
Precipitated from the driving-board,
Lifted their voices to bewail the youth
Who did such feats, and met with such hard fate,
Now dashed upon the ground, now seen with limbs
All upward flung to heaven; till chariot-men
Hardly restrained the steeds in their career,
And loosed him, bathed in blood, so that no friend,
Seeing the poor body, could have known 'twas he.
Then certain Phocians, ordered for the task,
Straightway consumed it on a funeral pile,
And hither in a little urn they bring
That mighty stature, in poor embers now,
To win a tomb in his own fathers' land.
Such is my tale; right piteous in the telling;
But in the sight of us, who witnessed it,
The saddest thing of all I ever saw.

1 LADY.   Alack, the lineage of our lords of old
Is all, too plainly, ruined from the root.

CLYTÆMNESTRA.   O God, this fortune — shall I call it fair,
Or black, though profitable? yet is it hard

That I should save my own life, through misfortunes
Which are my own!

GUARDIAN.   Why thus regretful, lady,
At what I have just told you?

CLYTÆMNESTRA.   It is strange —
This motherhood; for sons of one's own bearing,
However ill entreated at their hands,
One cannot muster hatred.

GUARDIAN.   I am come,
It seems, in vain.

CLYTÆMNESTRA.   Nay indeed, not in vain.
Why should you say in vain? if you are come
With a sure token that the man is dead,
Who was indeed the offspring of my being,
But from this bosom and maternal care
Revolted, and became as one estranged,
An exile; never, from the day he left
This country, saw me more; but, laying to me
His father's death, was ever threatening me,
So that sweet sleep by neither night nor day
Would cover me, but the impending hour
Held me continually in fear of death;
While now, since I am this day freed from terror
Of him, and of her too — for she dwelt with me
A far worse canker, ever draining deep
My very life-blood — now, for all her menaces,
I shall dwell tranquil!

ELECTRA.   O me miserable!
Why now, Orestes, there is room enough
To groan for thy misfortune, when, being thus,
Thou art scorned by this thy mother! Is it well?

CLYTÆMNESTRA.   Not thou — but he being as he is, is well.

ELECTRA.   Hear, Nemesis* of him who is no more!

CLYTÆMNESTRA.   Those she should hear Nemesis did hear, and well
   Did she perform!

ELECTRA.   Triumph! you are happy now.

CLYTÆMNESTRA.   You and Orestes cannot hinder me.

ELECTRA.   'Tis we are hindered; far from hindering you.

CLYTÆMNESTRA.   I were beholden to your coming, friend,
   If you could hinder her from her loud clamour.

GUARDIAN.   Well then, I will be going — if all is well.

CLYTÆMNESTRA.   Nay, for it were unworthy both of me
   And of the friend who sent you, did you meet
   Such entertainment. Please you enter in?
   Leave her alone, to sorrow out of doors
   For her dear friends' misfortunes, and her own.
                    [*Exeunt* CLYTÆMNESTRA *and Guardian.*

ELECTRA.   Seems it to you as if, in grief and pain,
   She was lamenting, weeping sore — the wretch!
   Over her son, thus lost? She is gone smiling!
   O me unhappy! Orestes, O my darling,
   How has thy death undone me! Parting thus,
   Thou tearest all the hopes out of my heart —
   All I had left — that thou would'st come, some day,
   Living, avenger of thy father's death,
   And of my wrongs. Now, whither should I turn?
   I am alone; I have no father; now
   I have not thee. Must I be slave once more
   Among the most detested of mankind,
   My father's murderers? Is it well with me?
   Nay, for the future never more at all
   Shall one roof hold us; rather, on this door-stone, friendless
   I will sink down and wear away and die!
   For this if any of the tribe within

---

* Another, more famous, goddess of revenge.

Is angered, let him kill me; death were welcome;
Life is but pain, and I am sick of it.

I. 1.

1 LADY.   Where be Jove's thunders, where the flaming Day,
    If, seeing these things, they hide them, and are still?

ELECTRA.   Ah, welaway!

1 LADY.   My child, why weepest thou?

ELECTRA.   Fie then —

1 LADY.   Speak gently.

ELECTRA.   Thou wilt slay me.

1 LADY.   How?

ELECTRA.   Yea, in my wasting, thou wilt trample more
    Upon me, if thou wilt suggest a hope
    For those who manifestly are dead and gone.

I. 2.

1 LADY.   I know that women's gold-bound toils ensnared
    The king Amphiaraus;* and now beneath —

ELECTRA.   Ah well a day!

1 LADY.   He reigns, with all his powers.

ELECTRA.   Ah, woe!

1 LADY.   Woe, for the murderess —

ELECTRA.   Slain?

1 LADY.   Ay, slain.

ELECTRA.   I know it, I know it; a champion was revealed
    For him, in trouble; none is left, for me;

---

* A reluctant participant in the mission of the Seven Against Thebes who was tricked by his
wife Eriphyle into joining up. Departing, he put a curse upon her which his own son later
fulfilled by killing her.

He who yet was is taken from me, and gone.

II. 1.

1 LADY.   Thou art meet for pity; piteous is thy lot.

ELECTRA.   That know I well, too well; my life is full
With month on month, with surge on surge of woes,
Hateful and fearful.

1 LADY.   All thy groans we know.

ELECTRA.   Therefore no more dissuade me, since not one —

1 LADY.   How say'st thou?

ELECTRA.   Is left of all my hopes of aid,
From him, the heir, born of one birth with me.

II. 2.

1 LADY.   All have their fate.

ELECTRA.   Meet all such fate as his,
Dragged in a cleft of the reins, poor hapless one,
Among fleet emulous hoofs?

1 LADY.   Strange, the mishap!

ELECTRA.   How otherwise, when without care of mine,
A stranger —

1 LADY.   Out, alas!

ELECTRA.   He passed away,
Meeting no burial, no lament, from me.

Enter CHRYSOTHEMIS.

CHRYSOTHEMIS.   My dearest, I am driven, for delight,
To throw decorum to the winds, and run!
For I bring pleasure, and an end of ills
You suffered from before, and sorrowed for.

ELECTRA.   Whence would you fetch assistance for my woes,
Whereof all healing is impossible?

CHRYSOTHEMIS.   Orestes is at hand! I tell you so!
He's here, in sight, plainly as you see me!

ELECTRA.   Fie, are you frantic, wretch, and do you jest
At your own sorrows, and at mine?

CHRYSOTHEMIS.   Not I,
By the house-altar! I do not say this
For wantonness; but he is come, indeed!

ELECTRA.   O wretched that I am! and from whose mouth
Did you receive this tale, that you believe
So over fondly?

CHRYSOTHEMIS.   It is proved to me
By my own eyes, none other; for I see
Clear evidence.

ELECTRA.   See proof? O wretch, what proof?
What did you see, to inflame you all at once
With this mad fever?

CHRYSOTHEMIS.   Listen, in Heaven's name,
That you may learn; and call me, afterwards,
Crazed, if you like, or sober.

ELECTRA.   Say your say,
If it affords you any pleasure.

CHRYSOTHEMIS.   I
Am telling you exactly what I saw.
As I approached our sire's ancestral grave,
I observed streams upon the pillar's top
Of milk fresh-running, and the sepulchre
Circled with garlands of all flowers in bloom.
I was surprised to see it, and looked round,
To see that no one near laid hand on me.
But when I found all quiet about the place,

I crept up to the tombstone, and perceived,
Upon the very corner of the pile,
A severed ringlet of a young man's hair.
No sooner did I see it, than there darts
Into my heart an image — ah! well known,
This that I was beholding was the token
Of my most dear Orestes! No light word
I uttered; but I took it in my hands,
And my eyes filled with tears at once, for joy.
And well I know, and well I knew it then,
How from no other came that ornament.
For whose work should it be, save yours or mine?
And I at least, I am certain, did it not,
Nor yet did you; how could you? when you know
You cannot even with impunity
Go out of doors to worship at a shrine;
Nor can it be our mother who would care
To do it, or have done it unperceived.
No, 'twas Orestes made those offerings.
But O dear heart, take courage! The same Power
Succours not always the same side alike;
And on us twain it has frowned hitherto;
But none the less, this morning shall be fraught
With many things for good.

ELECTRA.   Alack the while!
How I pity you for your folly!

CHRYSOTHEMIS.   But what is it?
Do I not speak to please you now?

ELECTRA.   You know not
Whither you are borne — how far you are astray!

CHRYSOTHEMIS.   But how can I not know, what I saw plainly?

ELECTRA.   O wretched girl, he's dead! his saving us
Is done and ended; never look to him!

CHRYSOTHEMIS.   Alas for pity! Who was it told you so?

ELECTRA.   One that was present with him, when he perished.

CHRYSOTHEMIS.   'Tis very strange. Where is he?

ELECTRA.   In the house;
Welcome, not odious, in our mother's eyes.

CHRYSOTHEMIS.   Alas for pity! But from whom, then, came
All those oblations to our father's grave?

ELECTRA.   I think most likely some one put them there
In memory of Orestes, who was dead.

CHRYSOTHEMIS.   O miserable! and I was hastening hither,
Joyful to have such tidings, unaware
What mischief was upon us! Now, arrived,
I find the old sorrows still, with others new.

ELECTRA.   'Tis so indeed; but if you list to me,
You can relieve the burden of the woe
Weighing on us now.

CHRYSOTHEMIS.   What, can I raise the dead?

ELECTRA.   That is not what I said; I am not so senseless!

CHRYSOTHEMIS.   What do you bid me, that is in my power?

ELECTRA.   Dare to do that which I shall urge on you!

CHRYSOTHEMIS.   If it will aid us, I shall not refuse.

ELECTRA.   Look, without effort nothing thrives.

CHRYSOTHEMIS.   I know it.
All I have strength for I will help to bear.

ELECTRA.   Hear, then, the course I am resolved upon.
Friends to stand by us even you must know
That none are left us; but the Grave has taken
And reft them; and we two remain alone.
I, while I heard my brother was alive
And well, had hopes that he would come, one day,

To the requiting of his father's death;
But since he is no more, to you I look
Not to refuse, with me, your sister here,
To slay the author of that father's murder,
Ægisthus; (we need have no secrets, now.)
For whither — to what still surviving hope
Do you yet look, and suffer patiently?
Who for the loss of your ancestral wealth
Have cause for grieving, and have cause for pain
At all the time that passes over you,
Growing so old, a maiden and unwed.
And these delights no longer hope to gain
At any time; Ægisthus is too prudent
To suffer that your progeny or mine
Should see the light, to his own clear undoing!
While, if you will be guided by my counsels,
First, you shall have the praise of piety
From your dead sire and brother in the grave,
Next, shall be called hereafter, as at first,
Free, and obtain a marriage worthy of you
For all men pay regard to honesty.
And as for glory — see you not what glory
You will confer upon yourself and me,
If you should heed me? For what citizen
Or stranger, who beholds us, will not greet
Our passing steps with praises such as these:
"Friends, look at those two sisters, who redeemed
Their fathers' house; who, prodigal of life,
Were ministers of slaughter to their foes
Who prospered well before; to them be worship,
To them the love of all men; at high feasts,
In general concourse, for their fortitude,
That pair let all men honour." Of us two
Such are the things that every man will say,
So that our glory shall not cease from us,
Living or dead. O, be persuaded, dear!
Succour your father's, aid your brother's cause,

Liberate me from evils, and yourself,
Remembering this, that a dishonoured life
Is shame to those who have been born in honour.

I LADY.   In work like this forethought is serviceable
Both to the speaker and the listener.

CHRYSOTHEMIS.   And if she were not mentally perverse,
She would have had some thought of prudence, ladies,
Before she ever spake — which now she has not.
Why, in what prospect do you arm yourself
With such a valour, and call me to aid?
Can you not see, you are not man, but woman?
Your hand is weaker than your enemies'.
Heaven sends good fortune daily upon them,
Which runs from us, and comes to nothingness.
Who, then, that schemed the death of one so mighty,
Could scape uninjured by calamity?
Look that we do not happen on worse ills,
Ill as we fare, if some one hears these sayings.
Death, with disgrace, though we obtain some credit,
Is no advantage and no help to us;
For death is not the worst; rather, in vain
To wish for death, and not to compass it.
But I beseech you, ere we are destroyed
With a complete destruction utterly,
Ere you abolish our whole family,
Set bounds on passion! What you said just now
I will keep close, unspoken, unensued;
Only be wise enough to yield at length
To stronger power, having yourself no strength.

I LADY.   Let her persuade you; there is no good thing
Better than foresight and sobriety.

ELECTRA.   You have said nought I did not look for. Well
I knew, you would reject my instances.
Yes, I must do it by myself alone;
At least, without one blow, we will not leave it.

CHRYSOTHEMIS.   Ah, would you had been so minded, when our sire
   Was murdered! Then you would have ended all!

ELECTRA.   I was, in temper; I lacked wisdom then.

CHRYSOTHEMIS.   Try and remain as wise for evermore!

ELECTRA.   Now that you preach, I know you will not help me!

CHRYSOTHEMIS.   And any man would come to harm who did!

ELECTRA.   I envy you your prudence; for your cowardice,
   I hate you!

CHRYSOTHEMIS.   I will bear it, when you praise.

ELECTRA.   Only you never will get praise of me!

CHRYSOTHEMIS.   It will be long, yet, before that is settled.

ELECTRA.   There is no service in you; get you gone.

CHRYSOTHEMIS.   There is! With you there is no towardness.

ELECTRA.   Go to your mother; tell it all to her.

CHRYSOTHEMIS.   Nay, I am not so much your enemy.

ELECTRA.   Do not forget, though, to what shame you drag me.

CHRYSOTHEMIS.   Shame not at all; but forethought for your good.

ELECTRA.   So I must follow what you think is just?

CHRYSOTHEMIS.   When you are prudent, you shall guide us both.

ELECTRA.   Pity that you should speak so well, and miss it!

CHRYSOTHEMIS.   You have named right the fault on your own side.

ELECTRA.   How can that be? Do you deny the justice
   Of what I say?

CHRYSOTHEMIS.   Justice sometimes brings damage.

ELECTRA.   Under those laws I do not choose to live

CHRYSOTHEMIS.   Well, you will find me right, if you will do it.

ELECTRA.   Ay and I will! You cannot frighten me.

CHRYSOTHEMIS.   Is't really so? Will you not change your mind?

ELECTRA.   Nothing's more odious than an evil mind.

CHRYSOTHEMIS.   You seem to care for nothing I can say.

ELECTRA.   I have resolved to do it of old time,
     Not newly.

CHRYSOTHEMIS. I am going. Neither you
     Deign to approve my words, nor I your ways.

ELECTRA.   Go in, then! I shall never follow you;
     Not though you come to wish it earnestly;
     There were small sense in running after — folly!

CHRYSOTHEMIS.   And if you think that reason is with you,
     So reason still! for, when your footsteps light
     In evil ways, then you will find me right.
                              [*Exit* CHRYSOTHEMIS.

CHORUS.

I.   I.

We that regard
The excellent wisdom of the birds of air,
     Who for the nurture care
Of those they spring from — those who gave them food,
     Why is it hard
For us, like them, to render good for good?
But, by the thunderbolt of sovereign Jove,
     And Themis, throned above,
          We scape not long!
Thou, who to mortals in the realms of death
Passest through earth, send forth thy voice, O Fame,
With piteous cry, to Atreus' sons beneath,
     Bearing thy tale of shame
          Unmeet for song.

I.   2.

How first of all
Corruption dwells within their palace hall,
        And, with their children, strife;
The dissonant watchword harmonized no more
            Now, as before,
By sweet endearments of their household life.
Electra, left alone, by rude waves tossed,
        Mourns for her father lost
            With ceaseless wail,
Even as the ever-sorrowing nightingale,
Careless for death, so she might end them too,
The accursed pair — yea, ready for the gloom;
        What woman lives as true
            This side the tomb?

II.   1.

For none among the great
        Would court oblivion,
Darkening his honour by a life of pain,
        As thou, my child, hast done,
        Choosing to share a fate
Full of all tears, not caring to obtain
At once, in the same breath, the twofold prize
Of daughter perfect, and of maiden wise.

II.   2.

Live thou — in wealth and force
        Above thy foes as far
As now thou dwellest underneath their might!
        For under no good star
        Have I held the course
Lying, of thy life; yet in the paths of Right

Most sovereign — thou, I say, in these hast trod
The foremost, through thy piety to God.

Enter ORESTES *and* PYLADES, *with an urn.*

ORESTES.   Were we told right, and are we tending right,
As we desire, fair ladies?

I LADY.   And what seek you?
What are you here for?

ORESTES.   I was asking where
Ægisthus lodged.

I LADY.   Then you are well arrived,
And your informant blameless.

ORESTES.   Which of you
Would kindly carry word to those within
Of the long-looked-for presence of us twain?

I LADY.   If the most near ought to announce it, she will.

ORESTES.   Lady, go in and tell them certain Phocians
Seek for Ægisthus.

ELECTRA.   O me miserable!
Are you not bringing tokens to confirm
The tale we heard?

ORESTES.   I do not know your story;
But my old master, Strophius, gave me charge
To tell about Orestes.

ELECTRA.   O sir, what?
How terror creeps upon me!

ORESTES.   We bring home
Poor relics of him, in a narrow urn,
Dead, as you see.

ELECTRA.   Unhappy that I am!

Here is the thing already evident.
I see your burden, I suppose, at hand.

ORESTES.   If you are grieving for Orestes' ills,
Know, that this vessel holds the dust of him.

ELECTRA.   O sir, in Heaven's name give it — if this urn
Hides him indeed — into my hands, to hold,
That I may weep and mourn to the uttermost
For my own self, and my whole race, at once,
Over these ashes!

ORESTES.   Bring it here, and give her,
Whoever she may be; for I am sure
She does not ask it out of enmity,
But as some friend, or blood-relation born.

ELECTRA.   Ah thou memorial of my best-beloved,
All that is left me of Orestes, how
Do I receive thee back — not as I hoped,
When I first sped thee on thy way! For now
I bear thee in my hands, and thou art nothing;
But O my child, I sent thee forth from home
Glorious with life! Would that I first had died,
Before I sent thee to a foreign land,
Stolen by these hands and out of slaughter saved;
So had that day beheld thee lying dead,
Partaking with me in thy father's grave.
But now thou hast perished — perished miserably,
An exile in a strange land, far from home,
Far from thy sister; nor with loving hands
Bathed I thy body, and laid it out — woe's me!
Nor, as was fitting, from the blazing pyre
Took up the poor remains. But cared for — ah,
By unfamiliar hands thou art come hither,
A little burden, in a little urn.
Ah me unhappy for my ancient care
Made fruitless, for the pleasing toil I spent,
Often, on thee! for not at any time

Wert thou thy mother's darling, more than mine;
I was thy nurse; no houselings fostered thee;
I was thy "sister," ever, too, by name.
But now all this has vanished in a day,
Even with thy death. For thou hast gathered all
Together, like a whirlwind, and art gone;
My father is no more; I too am dead
In thee; thyself art dead, and gone from me;
And our foes laugh; and that disnatured mother,
Of whom thou hast often sent word privily
Thou would'st thyself appear to punish her,
Raves with delight! This the ill Destiny
Of thee and me wrested away; who sent thee
On to me thus — not the dear form I loved,
But embers, and an unavailing shade.
— Woe's me! O piteous sight! Alas, alas,
A terrible journey hast thou gone, my dear;
Woe's me! and without thee I am undone;
I am undone without thee, O my brother!
Receive me then into this house of thine,
Nought unto nought, to dwell with thee below
For evermore. For when thou wast on earth,
All that I had on earth I shared with thee;
And — for I see no grieving in the dead —
I would die now, so I might share thy tomb.

I LADY.   Your sire, Electra, was a mortal man;
So was Orestes; wherefore do not grieve
Beyond all bounds; we all owe Heaven a death.

ORESTES.   O Heavens, what shall I say? whither shall I turn
For lack of words? for I have lost the power
Of speech!

ELECTRA.   What ails you? Wherefore do you say it?

ORESTES.   Is this the illustrious Electra — you?

ELECTRA.   That is it, and in case right miserable.

ORESTES.   Alack therefore, for this thy wretched lot!

ELECTRA.   Sir, you are not lamenting thus for me?

ORESTES.   O beauty foully — impiously destroyed!

ELECTRA.   The wretch you speak of is no other, sir,
Than I.

ORESTES.   Alas for thy estate, unwed,
Unfortunate!

ELECTRA.   Why do you groan, sir, thus,
Gazing on me!

ORESTES.   How did I nothing know
Of my own woes!

ELECTRA.   By what, that has been said,
Did you discover that?

ORESTES.   By seeing you,
Preëminent in multitude of griefs.

ELECTRA.   And yet you see but little of my woes.

ORESTES.   How could there be worse things than these to see?

ELECTRA.   That I am sorted with the murderers.

ORESTES.   Whose murderers? Whence is this hint of crime?

ELECTRA.   My father's. Next, I am perforce their slave.

ORESTES.   Who is it bends you to this exigence?

ELECTRA.   My mother — in name — but nothing mother-like.

ORESTES.   And how? by force, or wearing injury?

ELECTRA.   By force, by wearing, and all ills that be.

ORESTES.   And was none by to help or hinder it?

ELECTRA.   No; him I had you have brought here in ashes.

ORESTES.   Ill-fated one, how has the sight of you
Moved my compassion!

ELECTRA.   Know, you are the first
Who ever had compassion upon me.

ORESTES.   Because I am the first to come, who feel
With your misfortunes.

ELECTRA.   It can never be
You are some kinsman, who have come — whence could you?

ORESTES.   If these are friends about us, I will tell.

ELECTRA.   Yes, they are friends; you parley to safe ears.

ORESTES.   Put down this vessel, now, and learn the whole.

ELECTRA.   Ah sir, for Heaven's sake urge not this on me!

ORESTES.   Do as I tell you, and you shall not err.

ELECTRA.   Now, I adjure you, do not take away
My greatest treasure!

ORESTES.   I will not let you hold it.

ELECTRA.   O my Orestes! Woe is me for thee,
If I must be deprived of burying thee!

ORESTES.   Do not speak rashly. You do wrong to mourn.

ELECTRA.   How wrong, in mourning for my brother dead?

ORESTES.   It is not meet that you should call him so.

ELECTRA.   Am I then so disdained of him that's dead?

ORESTES.   Disdained of none; but you have no part here.

ELECTRA.   Not when I bear Orestes' ashes?

ORESTES.   Not
Orestes' ashes; only his in feigning.

ELECTRA.   Then where is that poor body's sepulchre?

ORESTES.   No where. The living have no sepulchre!

ELECTRA.   What say you, fellow?

ORESTES.   What I say is true.

ELECTRA.   Is he alive?

ORESTES.   Yes, unless I am dead!

ELECTRA.   What, are you he?

ORESTES.   See here, my father's seal!
Look at it well, and learn if I speak truly.

ELECTRA.   O happy day!

ORESTES.   Most happy; even so.

ELECTRA.   O art thou come, dear voice?

ORESTES.   No more to sound
From alien lips.

ELECTRA.   What, have I got you?

ORESTES.   Yes,
For you to keep, in future, evermore.

ELECTRA.   O dearest friends! O ladies, neighbours! Look,
Here is Orestes, only dead in craft,
And by that craft alive and safe at home!

1 LADY.   Daughter, we see it; and the tears of joy
Steal from our eyes, at what has come to pass.

ELECTRA.   O son, dear seed
Of one most dear to me!
And art thou come indeed?
Thou hast found—hast come, hast seen those thou didst
seek to see!

ORESTES.   Yes, I am here; but hush, keep silence.

ELECTRA.   Why?

ORESTES. Best to keep close, lest some one hear indoors.

ELECTRA. Nay but, by the ever-virgin Artemis,
    I never think to quail again at this,
    The cumbering plague of numbers feminine,
       That ever swarm within!

ORESTES. O but remember that in women too
    There lives a spirit of war; and thou hast proved it.

ELECTRA. Ah well a day!
    Thou makest the memory plain —
    That will not pass away —
       That cannot be forgotten — of my pain.

ORESTES. Sister, I know it; but, when occasion speaks,
    Then is it we should call to mind these doings.

ELECTRA. All day, all night,
    Were not too much for me
    To speak of them aright;
       Now that my lips at last are set at liberty.

ORESTES. I say not nay; therefore take heed.

ELECTRA.   Of what?

ORESTES. Now 'tis no time for talk, be sparing of it.

ELECTRA. Who, after thy appearing, would exchange
    Language for silence? That were dearly bought,
    Now I have found thee, in a manner strange
       Beyond all hope or thought!

ORESTES. You saw me then, when the Gods urged my coming.

ELECTRA. O grace, far more
    Than that thou first didst tell!
    If to thy kinsmen's door
       God sent thee safe, that count I miracle!

ORESTES. I am unwilling to restrain your joy,
    But fear you are too much overcome with rapture.

ELECTRA.   Oh, if after years of waiting
I have found thee condescending
By a way full fraught with blessing
   Here before me to appear,
Seeing me so full of troubles,
Spare, O spare —

ORESTES.   What should I spare thee?

ELECTRA.   Be not thou so much my wronger
As to make me lose the pleasure
Of thy presence!

ORESTES.   Nay,
I should be very wroth with other men
If I beheld them —

ELECTRA.   Do you say so?

ORESTES.   How
Could I forbear?

ELECTRA.   Hark, the voice, women dear,
I had never hoped to hear!
Listening, how could I have heard,
And held my peace, without one word,
Sorrowing? But I have thee, now!
With most sweet face there standest thou,
Face, that even in misery
Could not pass away from me.

ORESTES.   Pass what need not be said; spare me the telling
How base our mother; how Ægisthus drains
The family substance, giving largess here,
There scattering without purpose; for the tale
Would keep you from the occasion time has given.
But what will fit the present urgency,
Where, either visible or from ambushment,
We may give pause in this day's enterprise

To foes who mock, explain; be careful, too,
That as we enter at the palace door
Your mother do not spy your secret out
In your glad aspect; but be sighing, still,
As at that fiction of calamity;
For when we are successful, we shall be
Free to rejoice and laugh ungrudgingly.

ELECTRA.   Well, brother, as it pleases you in this,
So too shall be my pleasure; for from you
I have derived the blessings I enjoy—
Blessings not mine; and I could never bear,
By causing you annoy, ever so brief,
To reap great gain myself; for ill should I
So minister to the Providence at hand.
You know, no doubt, all that is passing here;
You heard Ægisthus was away from home,
My mother in the palace; and for her,
Fear not she will perceive my countenance
Radiant with smiles; for my long-standing hate
Is well worn in; and, having seen thy face,
I shall not leave off weeping now, for joy.
How should I leave it? who in this day's work
Saw thee first dead, then living! Yea, thou hast wrought
Very strangely with me; so that if my sire
Were to come here in life, I should not now
Deem it a marvel, but believe I saw him.
Since then by such a road thou art come hither
Lead on, as thou art minded; for alone
One of two things I had not failed to achieve—
Bravely to right myself, or bravely perish.

I LADY.   Peace, I advise you; for of those within
I hear one coming outward.

ELECTRA.   Enter, sirs;
The rather that you bring—what none would drive
Far from their doors—or willingly receive!

Enter Guardian.

GUARDIAN.   O most unwise and impotent of mind,
        Have you no longer any care to live,
        Or is no natural prudence bred in you,
        When in the very midst of ills most great,
        Not on their verge, you stand, and do not see it?
        If I had not been keeping, all along,
        Watch at the door-posts, all your business here
        Would have forestalled your presence in the house;
        But as it is, I took good heed of that.
        Now make an end of your long conference,
        And this insatiate crying out for joy,
        And pass within; for in such work as this
        Delay is loss, and it is time to finish.

ORESTES.   What will the issue be, if I go in?

GUARDIAN.   All's well so far, that you are quite unknown.

ORESTES.   You told them, I suppose, that I was dead?

GUARDIAN.   You'd think you were in Hades, though alive,
        To hear them talk!

ORESTES.   Do they rejoice at that?
        What are they saying?

GUARDIAN.   When the time is ripe
        I will inform you; but as things are now,
        All they are doing, however ill, goes well.

ELECTRA.   Brother, who is this man? For Heaven's sake, tell me!

ORESTES.   Do you not know him?

ELECTRA.   I cannot even guess.

ORESTES.   Not him, to whom you once delivered me?

ELECTRA.   What man? what do you mean?

ORESTES.   Him, in whose hands

I was made off with to the Phocians' land
By your providing?

ELECTRA.   What, is this the man
Whom only I found faithful out of many
When our sire perished?

ORESTES.   Once for all, 'tis he.

ELECTRA.   O happy day! O only saviour
Of Agamemnon's house! How art thou come hither!
Art thou the man who out of many woes
Didst save both him and me? O hands most dear!
O feet, most grateful for your ministry!
How could'st thou so long hide thee in my presence,
And kill me with false words, and shew me not,
Knowing all the while, the sweet reality?
O welcome, father! in thee I seem to see
A father! Welcome! Surely of all men thee
Within one day I have hated most—and love!

GUARDIAN.   Enough, I say; the story of all since then
Many revolving nights and days as many
Shall make to pass before Electra's eyes. —
But now I warn you both, you who stand by,
This is the time to act; now Clytæmnestra
Is left alone; now no one of the men
Is within doors; but if you will delay,
Consider, you will have to cope with these,
And more besides, and of more wit, than they.

ORESTES.   This need not be a matter to us now
For any long discoursing, Pylades!
Rather, first worshipping the ancestral shrines
Of all the Gods who keep this vestibule,
As quickly as we may, let us pass in.
                      [*Exeunt* ORESTES, PYLADES *and Guardian.*

ELECTRA.   O King Apollo, hear them graciously,
And me as well; me, who have come to thee

Right often, with persistent hand, that gave
Of all I had; so now with all I have,
Apollo, King Lycean, I implore,
I supplicate, I pray thee — go before,
And help us to our ends; and make mankind confess
How the Gods quit them, for their wickedness!   [*Retires.*

CHORUS.

I.

Behold where Ares, breathing forth the breath
   Of strife and carnage, paces — paces on.
The inevitable hounds of death,
   Hunters upon the track of guilt, are gone.
They stand the roof beneath;
And now not long the vision of my prayer
Shall tarry, floating in the fields of air.

2.

For now within these walls, with stealthy pace,
   The aider of the kingdoms of the dead
To his ancestral dwelling-place,
   Bearing keen slaughter in his hands, is led.
Hermes, of Maia's race,
Hiding his toils in darkness, leads the way
Straight to the goal, and makes no more delay.

ELECTRA (*advancing*).   O dearest women, 'tis the moment, now,
   For them to do the deed; but hush, keep still.

I LADY.   How then? What are they doing?

ELECTRA.   She is dressing
   The urn for burial; and the Pair stand by.

I LADY.   And what did you rush out for?

ELECTRA.   To take care

Ægisthus come not in without our knowing.

CLYTÆMNESTRA (*within*).   Woe's me! Alack, the house —
Empty of friends, and filled with murderers!

ELECTRA.   A cry within! O friends, do not you hear it?

1 LADY.   I heard, unhappy, sounds I might not hear;
And I am chill with horror.

CLYTÆMNESTRA (*within*).   Woe is me!
Ægisthus, O where are you?

1 LADY.   Hark again,
Some one is shrieking loud.

CLYTÆMNESTRA (*within*).   O child, my child,
Have mercy on your mother!

ELECTRA.   Thou hadst none
On him, or on his father who begat him.

CHORUS.

O city, O race ill-starred!
The curse is ever on thee, day by day,
To fade, and fade!

CLYTÆMNESTRA (*within*).   O, I am smitten!

ELECTRA.   If thou beëst a man,
Strike twice!

CLYTÆMNESTRA (*within*).   Again!

ELECTRA.   O for Ægisthus too!

CHORUS.

The curse is fulfilled.
They live, who lie in the grave.

> Slain long since, they drink, at last,
> The blood of their slayers, in turn.

I LADY.   See, they come forth! Their fingers drip with gore
Poured out on Ares' altar. I am dumb.

Enter ORESTES *and* PYLADES.

ELECTRA.   How is it with you, Orestes?

ORESTES.   In the house
Well; if Apollo's oracle be well.

ELECTRA.   Is the wretch dead?

ORESTES.   No longer be afraid
Thy mother's pride shall trample on thee more.

I LADY.   Cease, for I see Ægisthus full in view!

ELECTRA.   Back, boys!

ORESTES.   Where do you see the man?

ELECTRA.   He comes
Towards us from the precincts, gay at heart.

CHORUS.

> Make for the entrance, quick!
> Now, as ye have well achieved the former task,
> Finish this too!

ORESTES.   Be easy; we will do it.

ELECTRA.   Go your ways.

ORESTES.   I am gone.

ELECTRA.   I will provide for matters here.
                         [*Exeunt* ORESTES *and* PYLADES.

CHORUS.

'Twere well to pronounce
Brief words in this man's ear,
Mildly couched, that he may rush
On the hidden struggle of doom.

Enter ÆGISTHUS.

ÆGISTHUS.   Which of you knows, where are those Phocian strangers
They say have brought us tidings that Orestes
Has lost his life, by shipwreck of his team?
You there, my question is of you, yes, you
That used before to be so malapert;
For it concerns you most, I think, to know,
And more than all, it is for you to say.

ELECTRA.   I know. How could I help it? Otherwise
I should be ignorant of calamity
Nearest to me — of mine.

ÆGISTHUS.   And where may be
The strangers? tell me, pray.

ELECTRA.   They are within.
They — fell on a kind hostess!

ÆGISTHUS.   Did they say
That he is dead in very earnest?

ELECTRA.   Nay,
They brought and shewed it us — not merely told us.

ÆGISTHUS.   Is it hard by, that I may see, and know?

ELECTRA.   You may, indeed — a very sorry sight.

ÆGISTHUS.   Your words have pleased me much; which is not usual.

ELECTRA.   If they can give you pleasure, pray be pleased.

ÆGISTHUS.   Now hold your peace, and open wide the gates,
  For Myceneans, Argives — all to see,
  So that, if any of them heretofore
  Were buoyed by empty hopes of such an one,
  Seeing him now dead, they may accept my curb,
  And, having me for chastener, may not need
  To be compelled to bring forth fruits of wisdom!

ELECTRA.   It is all done, on my part; for at last
  I have the wit to choose the stronger side.

The scene opens, disclosing the body of CLYTÆMNESTRA, *veiled;*
  ORESTES *and* PYLADES *standing by.*

ÆGISTHUS.   Zeus, I behold a thing — that hath not fallen,
  But by the jealousy of Heaven! — Nay,
  If there is yet a Nemesis, I unsay it!
  Loosen all coverings from before my face,
  That of me too my kindred may obtain
  The meed of mourning.

ELECTRA.   Take them off yourself.
  To see this corpse, and speak with amity,
  Is not my work, but yours.

ÆGISTHUS.   Well, you say true,
  And I will do your bidding; in mean while,
  If she is in the house, call Clytæmnestra.

He raises the veil.

ORESTES.   Seek her no further; she is at your side.

ÆGISTHUS.   O what is this?

ORESTES.   Who is it, whom you fear?
  Who is it, whom you do not recognize?

ÆGISTHUS.   Who are the men into whose very toils
  I have fallen, unhappy?

ORESTES.   Did you never dream
   They were alive, whom you miscall as dead?

ÆGISTHUS.   O me, I understand you! It must be
   No other than Orestes speaks to me.

ORESTES.   Excellent seer! and yet so long deceived!

ÆGISTHUS.   I am lost, miserably! But suffer me
   To speak a little —

ELECTRA.   Brother, in Heaven's name let him
   No further parley, and prolong discourse.
   Once overtaken by calamity,
   What profit should a man who is to die
   Draw from delay? Nay, kill him on the spot,
   And cast him forth, slain, to such buriers
   As it is fitting he should meet withal,
   Out of our eye-sight! This alone can be
   An expiation for my wrongs of old.

ORESTES.   Go thou within, with speed. The contest now
   Lies not in words, but for thy life-blood.

ÆGISTHUS.   Nay,
   Why do you drag me to the house? What need
   Of darkness, if the deed is honourable?
   Why are you backward to despatch me here?

ORESTES.   Prescribe not thou! Pass, where thou slew'st my father,
   And perish there.

ÆGISTHUS.   Is it fated that this roof
   Must witness all the ills of Pelops' race,
   That are, or shall be?

ORESTES.   Thine, at any rate.
   I am soothsayer good enough to tell thee that!

ÆGISTHUS.   The craft you boast was not inherited, then!

ORESTES.   Thou prat'st, and prat'st; and the way lengthens out;
   Move on.

ÆGISTHUS.   Lead forward.

ORESTES.   Thou must foot it first.

ÆGISTHUS.   Lest I escape thee?

ORESTES.   Rather, that thy soul
    May not pass easily; this bitterness
    I must reserve for thee. And well it were
    If this quick justice could be dealt on all —
    Whoever will transgress the bounds of right,
    To strike him dead.   [*Kills* ÆGISTHUS.
           So should not villainy thrive.

CHORUS.

      O Atreus' seed!
  How hardly, after many labours past,
  Art thou come forth to liberty at last,
      Through this new trial perfected indeed!
                [*Exeunt omnes.*